On with the Show!

On with the Show!

A Guide for Directors and Actors

Sheri L. M. Bestor

Teacher Ideas Press
Portsmouth, NH

Teacher Ideas Press
A division of Reed Elsevier Inc.
361 Hanover Street
Portsmouth, NH 03801–3912
www.heinemann.com

Offices and agents throughout the world

Library of Congress Cataloging-in-Publication Data

Bestor, Sheri L. M.
  On with the show! : a guide for directors and actors / Sheri L. M. Bestor.
      p. cm.
    Includes bibliographical references and index.
    ISBN 1-59469-002-2 (alk. paper)
  1. Theater rehearsals. 2. Theater—Production and direction. 3. Acting. I. Title.
  PN2071.R45B47 2005
    792'.02'33—dc22   2004028490

Editor: Suzanne Barchers
Production Coordinator: Angela Rice
Typesetter: Westchester Book Services
Cover Design: Gaile Ivaska
Manufacturing: Steve Bernier

Printed in the United States of America on acid-free paper

09 08 07 06 05 ML 1 2 3 4 5

For Whitnie, Kaitilyn, and Hailie

For Scott

Contents

Reproducibles

Acknowledgments

I am grateful to: Bill S. Mabry, Founder of Rhodium Records, for his professional guidance in the industry; my colleagues and friends, including those at NSAA and in my critique group, and M.T.; my editor, Suzanne Barchers, for giving me this opportunity, and Karyn Slutsky, Angela Rice, and the staff at Teacher Ideas Press; my family, including my husband and children, my mom and dad, Bill and John, and GG, for their support; and the "Stagekids" who make it all worthwhile.

Introduction

"An hour of rehearsal for every minute of performance time"—this is the golden rule for producing a play or a musical. Both directors and actors know how precious rehearsal time is, that they can't waste a moment of it. This book will help directors and actors get the most out of rehearsal time at home and on the stage. It will aid in the process of working toward the production—strengthening skills while building confidence on the stage. It will provide the tools for cast members to reach their performance goals and allow directors to be as organized and efficient as possible so that all can enjoy the thrilling process of putting on a play or musical.

The book is divided into a director's handbook and an actor's handbook. The director's handbook is made up of explanatory chapters and a chapter with reproducibles. The explanatory chapters are arranged in the order in which a director runs through the production process, beginning with auditions and concluding with the performances. It is suggested that directors read through each chapter of this section, from start to finish, prior to auditions and the first rehearsal, and then refer back to each chapter when reaching that component of the rehearsal process. This section of the book includes an explanation of various charts and forms in Chapter 4 that are suggested for use, complete with samples of each. The samples will give you an idea of how a director would fill out each chart or form. Refer to this when determining how you can use the forms and charts.

Each chapter covers a different topic related to producing a show. Chapter 1 covers auditions, including tips on how to announce auditions, prepare for them, and conduct them. Chapter 2 covers all of the aspects of rehearsals, from creating attendance charts, to lesson plans, to keeping track of notes you create, to preparing your script for use. Chapter 3 discusses the actor's handbook, the use of the materials that you will be giving to the actors, and what you will be covering for each component of the production. It offers suggestions for helping your cast through the rehearsal process as well as how they can use the actor's handbook during the rehearsal process.

Chapter 4 of the director's handbook includes all of the reproducibles. They are labeled as they are referenced in the explanatory chapters. For example, the first chart mentioned is labeled DR1, which stands for director reproducible 1. These pages should be duplicated and kept in files or a binder under each corresponding heading. When preparing for auditions, create a file folder labeled auditions (specifying the show title) include all notes, forms, charts, and information that you create, use, and gather with regard to auditions. Do this for each component of the show and store these file folders in a portable file box. Keep this box with you during rehearsals and when you are planning.

Section 2 is written for the actor. It is the actor's handbook and should be duplicated for each cast member. Although the director should be familiar with the actor's handbook, this section is to be read by the actors.

There are two ways to use the actor's handbook. One is to duplicate the entire section (excluding the audition section, which should be given out prior to auditions) and bind it as a booklet by either three-hole punching it and keeping it in a binder or stapling it. You and your cast can go through the entire manual together during the first rehearsal. The director will explain to the cast how each chapter of the book works, specifying expectations. For instance, the director might assign the cast the task of completing their character studies prior to memorizing their lines.

The second method of use is to hand out each chapter of the actor's handbook when you are ready to address that topic. For example, when you want the cast to focus on characterization, hand out that chapter of the handbook. Age, maturity of the cast, and experience will help you to determine which method will work best for you and your cast.

Chapter 1 of the actor's handbook focuses on the audition process. Chapter 2 focuses on the at-site rehearsals. It discusses attendance, schedules, input of cast into rehearsals, preparing a script, preparing for rehearsals, and taking notes at rehearsals. It focuses on what cast members need to do at rehearsals while allowing the director time to cover the actual rehearsal plans.

Chapter 3 deals with how the cast should rehearse at home and includes forms and charts to facilitate such individual rehearsals. The final chapter discusses the show itself and the aftermath.

Having successful rehearsals is the key component to having a successful show in which all actors are self-confident and enjoy presenting their project. This book will make the rehearsal process run efficiently and smoothly for the director as well as the actor so that you can get "on with the show!"

Section 1

The Director's Handbook

As a director, you have to devise a rehearsal plan that allows enough time to introduce the major components of the show—blocking, dialogue, choreography, vocal, acting in character, and so forth—as well as pull those components together to produce a smooth running interpretation of the story you are trying to tell on stage. Concentrating on these major components allows little time to focus on the "method" of rehearsing. This book will help you integrate time-saving rehearsal tips and it will offer plans for your cast to work through rehearsal methods to ensure the best use of time to prepare for the best possible production.

Chapter 1

Auditions

Auditions are one of the most crucial yet stressful components of a production. A team relationship has not yet been established between the directors and actors, so often a division is felt between the panel of auditors (those judges who handle casting decisions) and the auditioning actor up on stage. This lack of synergy can have an impact on the final outcome of casting. However, the more information given to the auditioners (those actors auditioning for a part in a production) prior to auditions, the more the director "sets the scene" and is able to eliminate misconceptions about the process, or at least misconceptions about his or her specific style or casting that will impact the directing. This information will help ensure that actors can prepare for the specific audition and hone in on what the auditors will be seeking, making the auditions more efficient and successful.

Pre-audition Meeting

To establish an optimum audition scene, a pre-audition meeting is recommended. More often than not, directors will post an audition announcement and simply accept those interested into the audition roster. However, having a meeting for those interested in auditioning and sharing all pertinent information will have an impact on the success of auditions. If you allow a time for questions and a chance for the auditioners to meet the director in person, it will make the process less intimidating for the actors and give them a clearer vision of what you will be seeking at auditions.

Planning the Pre-audition Meeting

Set the meeting date with enough time between it and the actual auditions to allow actors ample time to prepare, as this will be the time in which you distribute the audition materials.

When announcing the pre-audition meeting, make sure to stress that you would like the parents or guardians, as well as the actors, to attend. This of course will depend on the age range of actors you are pulling from. Include the time, location, date, length of time the meeting will run for, and a list of the general information that will be shared during the meeting. Also, include a brief description of the production. An example of a pre-audition meeting form can be found in Chapter 4 of the director's handbook (see form DR1).

Keeping a Clear Count

Set a deadline for accepting audition registrants and post this date to the public. Stick to this cut-off date even though it is tempting to let stragglers sneak onto the roster. Although many directors permit "walk-ins" to audition, this makes it challenging to keep an organized record of who is auditioning and it makes the auditions run less efficiently. Although you may miss a few strong actors if you close auditions and don't allow walk-ins, soon enough people will learn the methods of your organization or school and come to know that they must register before the deadline to have an opportunity to audition.

Materials to Include in the Pre-audition Meeting

Prepare for the meeting by having enough materials available for everyone present (DR2). These materials should include:

Information about, and a description of, the show.

Where and when the show will be performed.

Information about the crew (directors and producers).

Specific cast requirements and information on what you are seeking, including double casting, and so forth.

Information about auditions (dates, time, procedure).

Information about preparation materials.

What auditors are seeking in auditions.

How auditions will be posted/announced.

Conducting the Meeting

Begin the meeting by passing out an agenda (DR3). Use the agenda to guide your meeting, but make notes on a master copy that you will use to run the meeting. It is not necessary to include specific details and information on the copies of the agenda you hand out to the actors and parents. Rather, discuss each point on the agenda so that parents must take notes and be involved in the meeting. This encourages focus and interest.

Introduce yourself and anyone else from the production staff who is present. Include your credentials. It is important that the auditioning talent (and their parents) develop respect for their director, and this is an opportune time to begin developing it. Turning to the agenda, briefly discuss the show and your excitement about it, giving those present at the meeting an insight into how you will use your creative directing style to make it a unique show. Hand out the production information sheet (DR4).

Next, discuss the value of the "process" of the experience. Make it clear that the process of rehearsals is as important as the production. Explain your goals for the program and what you hope your actors will gain from this enriching experience, including building self-esteem, forging friendships, working cooperatively as a team, and working with the community. Mention the other components of a major production, such as learning about characterization, blocking, choreography, and vocal technique. Make clear your expectations about rehearsals, attendance, memorization, and follow-through with responsibilities for the show. It may be necessary to provide a list of production policies that outline your expectations, such as procedures for missing a rehearsal (i.e., must have a signed note from a parent) and repercussions for those who miss several rehearsals (DR5). The more the cast knows ahead of time, the more you can enforce your standards throughout the production season.

Your Audition Expectations

Auditioners are anxious to learn the specifics of the show and what you are looking for as a director in auditions. Be as specific as you can without tying yourself to a situation in which your creativity will be stifled once the rehearsals begin due to previous announcements. It is important to discuss the qualifications of the auditors and what they will be seeking during this process. There is no need to mention specific names, but it is important to let the actors (and their parents) know that the judges are impartial and have no relationships with any of the auditioning actors. This would also be the time to mention if any of the roles of the show are going to be pre-cast. If you pre-cast an actor, be prepared to lose a possible better character fit from someone who might audition.

Hand out a character involvement chart for the roles you are seeking to fill (DR6). Using the script and score, indicate each character's involvement in the show by reviewing the musical/play and filling in the chart. Explain which roles involve singing, dancing, acting, or a combination of these, and specify the commitment of each part. Let the auditioners know the rehearsal schedule of the leads versus the chorus parts and the option of auditioning for one or the other or both.

The pre-audition meeting is the time to explain what type of audition is being held. Clarify whether they are role auditions—actors seek a specific part in the show—or general auditions—actors will be a part of the show and auditions help establish which part they will have. It is important to articulate clearly your expectations about casting results. What a setback it would be to cast an actor in a lead role and then to learn that he was only interested in a certain part (other than what he was cast as) and so refuses, in the end, to participate in the show at all. This can create a gap in the casting results, mandating further auditions, which can push off the start of rehearsals and have an impact on the success of the show, all before auditions have even been completed.

The "Meat" of the Meeting

Now for what everyone is truly waiting for—how to prepare for auditions and how auditions will be run.

Actors will be anxious to know if there will be cold readings, what they will need to sing, if there will be live accompaniment, if they will have a script given to them to rehearse and prepare with, and if they will be expected to do a choreography block during auditions. Explain in detail the procedure for auditions—what will happen first, second, and third. Specify what time to arrive, if there will be a group warm-up, and how auditions will be run. Hand out the audition information form (DR7) for actors to fill out and return the day of auditions, and let the auditioners know they need to bring a recent photo. Mention what will happen with callbacks and, finally, how audition results will be posted. Of course, allow enough time in the meeting for questions.

Specific information sets an actor at ease, especially those auditing for the first time, which will make it more likely that you will be able to see what he or she can truly do and portray, giving you a more accurate read of talent. Included in the actor's handbook section of this book is a set of handouts that will be helpful to auditioners. Use your discretion as to whether you would like to assist auditioners by handing out this information at the pre-audition meeting or if you would rather see what each auditioner brings on his or her own.

Distribute form DR8 to all auditioning students at the pre-audition meeting. It is designed to help students plan their practice time to prepare for auditions. To prepare for auditions, it is recommended that students rehearse at home each day leading up to the audition. This form is a way for students to record how much time they will set aside to prepare. It also gives students a way of investigating the parts they are auditioning for and a plan for how to be cast in the desired role.

A Good First Impression

Remember, this is the first exposure your actors (and their parents) will have to you, so look and act the part of an experienced, organized, and talented director. Strive to wrap up the meeting within the time you allotted. Make this first impression memorable. It is your job to make sure all actors who come to the pre-audition meeting leave still wanting to audition.

The Auditions: Casting the Show

Keeping the auditions organized and well run is one of the most important elements of auditions. Make sure your auditors are well prepared and that you have taken some time before the actors arrive to go over the procedures as well as the rating system so everyone is consistent when rating the auditioners (DR9).

When it is time to begin conducting auditions, have a "runner" who will call each auditioner into the room and accept their paperwork to be given to the auditors. Or, you might locate or invest in an intercom device that you can use to call specific actors into the audition room. In the case of a musical production, have music ready, whether it is a live pianist (ideal) or a tape or CD with the music recorded multiple times to avoid wasting time rewinding the cassette or finding the correct place on a CD. Go through the procedures with the group and then begin individual auditions. Make sure the actors are ready when you cue the music or ask them to begin reading. Make eye contact, be pleasant, and do not take any notes during the performance. Give the auditioner your undivided attention. It takes a lot of nerve and preparation to get up and audition, and these actors deserve this chance to prove to you what they can do for your show.

When an audition has concluded, hand the auditioner an audition slip (DR10), thank him or her in a positive manner, and communicate clearly that the audition is over. Further, make sure to remind auditioners where and when to find the casting results (DR11). You will most likely want to post the casting results in public for all to see. In addition, you may want to send letters to all students who auditioned to let them know the results. Depending on if everyone who auditions makes the cast or not, determine which type of letter you will send (DR12, DR13). You may also want the new cast members to sign commitment contracts, assuring that they will commit to the show for the benefit of all involved (DR14).

Chapter 2

Getting the Most Out of Rehearsals

Effective rehearsals are the key to a successful show. You can cast the twenty most talented, energetic, and experienced actors in the community or school, but if they don't dedicate the time and commitment needed to work through each aspect of the show, it simply will not be a success. If you as the director do not have a solid plan to work through the rehearsal process, much time will be wasted and you will enter production week unprepared.

Attendance

It is crucial that the cast take attendance seriously. You have ultimate control over what is accomplished at each rehearsal to prepare for the show, but unless the actors know the importance of the team concept and show up when they are supposed to, you might as well cancel rehearsal. It is challenging to hold a rehearsal if *any* of the actors are absent, because no one can get a good feel for the whole picture when part of that picture is missing. Therefore, from the onset, drive home to the cast the importance of showing up. Hand out a rehearsal schedule and be as specific as you can about what will be covered at rehearsals without locking yourself into something too rigid (DR15). If you can specify what you will be doing at each rehearsal, at least in general, then you can expect your cast to come prepared to each session. They will realize that if they don't attend, they will miss something important. Further, periodically explain the production policies to the cast, emphasizing the repercussions of missing rehearsals (DR5).

Rehearsal Attendance Schedule

You may want to consider dividing the cast up during rehearsals so that you can target certain parts of the show with only those actors who are involved. For example, you might work on three of the songs during one of the rehearsals and have only those students involved in them attend that particular rehearsal. This will help avoid cast members sitting around at rehearsals getting bored. This boredom can cause future poor attendance. If actors feel that they are not contributing at rehearsals and their time can be better spent elsewhere, they will be elsewhere—if not in body, then in mind. Another way to organize rehearsals is to have the entire cast and several directors present; while the vocal director is working with one group, the choreographer is working with another, and so on. This can be tricky to schedule but once done, it is a very effective way to rehearse and the cast appreciates keeping busy. Aside from the division of rehearsal groups, there are, of course, times when the entire cast should be called to rehearsal. However, try and streamline your rehearsal plans.

The most effective way to work up the attendance schedule is to create a chart by carefully going over the script and marking each scene that each character is to be present on stage (DR6). When putting together your rehearsal schedule, plan to cover sections in the show that call for the same actors. Be careful, however, to make sure to allow for straight run-through rehearsing, too, as it is vitally important to teach the cast how the flow of the entire show will be handled.

Rehearsal Lesson Plans

To put together an organized rehearsal plan, begin with a calendar in hand and move backwards from production date to the first rehearsal date, or visa versa. It will be your decision, based on the caliber of your actors and the complexity of the show, how many of each type of rehearsal you will actually need to plan (DR18a, b). Make sure to include in your plans the following types of rehearsals.

Read-throughs. The complete cast and crew should be present to read through the entire show and discuss the director's vision and concept. Each director of the various components of the show should have time to discuss his or her responsibility in the show (e.g., the costume director will explain costumes). In addition to the read-through rehearsal, the director needs to plan specific rehearsals to work with the cast. These rehearsals are in addition to choreography, vocal, and blocking rehearsals (DR16).

Vocal Rehearsals (for musicals only). The music should be introduced as one of the first components of the show. Have the cast become familiar with the music and delegate parts to each cast member so they know which parts to rehearse at home. It is best to give them a copy of the written (vocal score) and auditory (either a cassette or CD) music so that they can learn it quickly at home (DR19).

Blocking Rehearsals. Working through the physical aspects of the show on stage is beneficial to do while the students are learning their lines. Introduce stage business, the movement each character in a scene will complete, as well as the physical character interaction, such as characters greeting each other by shaking hands, and so on (DR20, DR21).

Choreography Rehearsals (for musicals only). The choreographer must work closely with the director to ensure that their respective blocking styles mesh. The choreographer needs to know the entrances and exits on stage in order to direct the onset of songs. It is crucial that the choreographer work closely with the vocal director as well. Together, they can establish the stage movement within each number. Choreography should be taught song by song at the onset of the rehearsal season to allow time for at-home rehearsals to perfect each number (DR22).

Work-throughs (off book). The cast should have the show learned without needing the assistance of the script fairly early on in the production season, but a line-feeder should be present at the early stage. The cast will run through the show line by line on stage, incorporating all blocking. Efforts should be taken to keep the show running as smoothly as possible, however, because dropping and forgetting lines can become tedious and frustrating for actors.

Run-throughs for Act 1. Work through the show scene by scene in act 1 to establish continuity, but interrupt the run-through as needed to fix and adjust troublesome areas of the show. All cast members who are involved in act 1 should be present.

Run-throughs for Act 2. Work through the show scene by scene in act 2 to establish continuity, but again, interrupt to fix and adjust troublesome areas of the show. All cast members who are involved in act 2 should be present.

Pick-up Rehearsals. These rehearsals are designed to be called for specific work needed on the show. If the rehearsals are running smoothly and everything is on schedule, pick-up rehearsal dates can be left open on the calendar for a "break" if necessary. It is crucial to make sure pick-up rehearsals are scattered throughout your schedule, putting in at least one per section of the rehearsal plan (one after choreography is taught, one after blocking is to be completed, and so forth). In this way, you are assured that the cast has time available in case extra rehearsing is needed. Again, referring back to the attendance, if you throw in an unannounced rehearsal, chances are high that you will only have a handful of cast members present and so, little will get accomplished, which makes it is very frustrating for those who do attend. If you have a pick-up rehearsal scheduled on the calendar, it will be more likely to have a good turn out.

Complete Run-through. Run the entire show from beginning to end. Make sure you have enough time allotted to run the length of the production so the age-old dilemma of act 1 being polished and act 2 never having a chance to be completed does not occur. When conducting the run-through, don't stop to give tips to the actors. Let them get a feel for the flow of the show while you attain a run time for the show as well. While you are observing the run-through, take specific, scene-by-scene notes. Afterward, have a meeting with the cast to discuss each component of the run-through as a large-group cast. Specific details that will not benefit the whole cast should be dealt with on an individual basis while the other cast members are taking a break. In your notes, code each comment as "large group" or "individual" so that you can discuss what is pertinent for whoever is present. Use the "Run-through" note page (DR25) or take notes per student (DR23).

Technical Rehearsals (including "tech only" rehearsals). All of the technical components of the show are put into place, including lights, sounds, special effects, and so on. These rehearsals are intense and call for sound checks, interruptions to adjust mics, and much more, so don't plan on combining a run-through with a technical rehearsal. It won't happen.

Dress Rehearsal. The show is run from beginning to end with all scenery changes, use of props, costume changes, curtain calls, technical components, and so on. It is the final run-through before opening night.

The rehearsal schedule should be clear, concise, and well documented (DR17). Think of it as trying to reach a destination by using the globe. First you get a whole picture (of the world), but then you start honing in, getting closer and closer to the destination (country, then state, then city) until you are approaching where you intend to reach—working on the very specifics of the show. By the end, you have reached your destination and can look around and enjoy the place at which you have arrived. Hopefully, this "place" is a well-rehearsed show that provides not only audience enjoyment, but also actors' pleasure in performing.

General Date and Time Schedule

When devising the time and dates for rehearsals, take into consideration not only what will be occurring at each rehearsal but also the needs of your cast and crew. Avoid scheduling rehearsals on school holidays, as many people will be away on family vacations. Do not schedule rehearsals on any type of holiday—you must think of all religions, not just the most popular. Avoid weekend evenings for rehearsals. Call as many rehearsals as you need, but don't over do it. Although your expectations of the dedication for all involved need to be clear, you can't expect this show to be the only focus in their lives.

Director's Notes

When watching a rehearsal, the more notes you can take—instead of interrupting and making corrections on the spot—the better. Use either of the charts included in the director's handbook: one is a page designed specifically for a cast member (DR23) so that the director's notes will be thoughts on students, one student per page; the other chart allows the director to take notes on each scene (DR24). Taking notes is helpful at the beginning of the rehearsal process, when the cast is just getting a feel for the production, or at the very end, when it is crucial for the cast to know the flow of the show. Consider taking notes to save time and keep the show moving. Jot down your thoughts. If a suggestion has to do with an actor, discuss it with the actor at the end of the rehearsal and have him or her document the note in the actor's handbook. Tell the cast member to work on this component of the show. You'll have your own copy of that direction so that during the next rehearsal, you can indicate if the problem has been taken care of (indicate if so on your copy) or not (revisit the actor). This book of notes is helpful even from one show to the next. You can refer back to it to see where your cast had the most trouble. You may be able to plan your rehearsals for the next show accordingly to give extra attention to areas that consistently need more work (i.e., group exits after a big choreography number) (DR25).

Script Preparation

Before anything else, you must prepare the script. Get one copy that you can write on and highlight, and then disassemble it. Take each page and put it on an 8½"×11" piece of paper. Three-hole punch all of the papers and put them in a binder. Add blank pages at the beginning of the book. Also, measure margins—the distance between the holes in the paper and the beginning of the text of the script. Make strips of paper this same width, three-hole punch them, and put one of these blank strips in front of each page.

Now you are ready to read through the script scene by scene. Take notes on your general vision, writing these notes down on the first full-sized blank pages. When you are ready to move on, start in on the specifics of the show. Use the margin note pages to jot down thoughts about stage entrances and exits, stage movement, blocking, and vision. Use the extra margin copy of paper to indicate all tech notes—lighting calls and sound, curtain calls, and scene changes. These tech margin pages can be used when you meet with your tech crew and when you do run-throughs. They can be flipped over when not in use so that you can access your notes on the specifics of the stage movement.

Indicate all notes in your script in pencil or use Post-it Notes. As you work through the production during rehearsals, you may need to make changes in your original plans.

In this binder, make sure to include an area at the back that includes a cast list, contact information for each cast member and crew member, your complete schedule, and a copy of each correspondence note you plan to send or do send home to your cast or crew.

If you cannot disassemble a script because it is only available for rental and can't be purchased, use the script page in the handbook to create notes that you will include after each page of the script (DR26).

When taking notes on choreography plans, blocking, stage business, and the like, it may be useful to use abbreviations for common terms to save not only space in your notes, but also time writing (DR27).

Remember, a director who is well organized can maximize rehearsal time so that the process, as well as the product, is effective and enjoyable for all involved.

Chapter 3

Coming to Rehearsals Prepared: The Student Handbook

Your cast is interested in doing the best they can to make the show a hit. They have worked hard preparing for auditions and are putting forth their best efforts at rehearsals. Now they need to begin working at home on the show, memorizing their lines, practicing the choreography they have been taught, and going over the blocking. If the cast is well prepared, much more can be accomplished at the rehearsals.

The problem comes when you tell the actors to rehearse at home and they stare back at you with the look of, "Okay, I'll do that, but how?" It seems second nature to natural born theater folks—just read through the script and learn your parts! What's the problem? But some, especially the younger or less experienced actors, are lost when they don't have a director in front of them. They may not have the discipline to set aside the practice time at home; they may misplace their scripts or not take accurate rehearsal notes; they may be at a loss for knowing how long to rehearse; and, most likely, they may simply not know how to go about learning what they need to learn. This is where the student section of this book is vitally important. Make sure to make copies of the section about at-home rehearsals and go over each component in class. You will want to make duplicate copies of the vocal, blocking, and choreography charts so that students can fill out a chart for each song, scene, set, and so on. You will find that the cast will come to rehearsal much more prepared because you have given them the tools to be successful.

Dialogue

Lines should not be learned during rehearsal; they should be learned at home. However, it is important for you as the director to give some indication as to how each character will deliver lines. Give examples and take this opportunity to do some enrichment teaching on acting. Discuss the importance of not sounding memorized. Your students should be taking notes in their booklets.

Getting into Character

Although all of the components added together make for a hit or failure of a production, getting into character is key in pulling the audience into the action of the show. If the cast can "act" as the characters they have been cast as, the show will be believable and, just like a good movie, it will make an impression on its audience. As the director, it is your job to make sure this type of characterization occurs. This must be one of the first things you get across to the actors, because how they learn the material will determine how they present it. Discuss memorization, acting with their full body, facial expression, and voice inflection. Make sure to give examples of acting that is dull and lifeless versus acting that is full of life and expression. Teach your cast about overacting and how not to seem melodramatic. The students should note all of these points in their books so that while they are at home rehearsing, they can review them and get the most out of their home rehearsal time.

One exercise to have your cast do is a characterization study. Have them go home and spend one week getting to know their characters. Is the character old, hard of hearing, young, vibrant, quick tempered, kind, soft spoken, slow, fast, happy, sad, and so on? The students must establish their characters based on the script, your input, and their imagination. And then they must work hard on learning how to get into character on stage and remain in character, consistently, for the remainder of the show. They should do their characterizing study in their rehearsal workbooks and then bring them back for your review.

If the cast effectively portrays their characters, they will enjoy the acting more and the audience will enjoy the show more. And when each of these parties picks up on this enjoyment, they feed off of each other and the result is a hit of a show!

Blocking

Blocking should be preplanned. You should have indications in your script on how you would like your actors blocked through each scene. Don't get up on stage during rehearsals and vacillate between blocking actions—you will lose not only the attention of your cast, but also their respect. That's not to say that you can't make subtle changes in blocking as you go along to improve the show. That's a big component of rehearsals. Just make sure to have a solid idea of the general blocking patterns you plan on introducing to your students.

When you are working through the blocking, have your cast use their blocking section of the handbook. They should carefully take notes. If they are literally working through the blocking on stage, they should pick up their books when they have a break in rehearsals and enter the information. Good blocking will help the cast learn their lines as well, because the lines—the meaning—should fit with the action the characters are doing. One will trigger the other.

Vocals

Music is an additional component for a production, and it demands that time be set aside in the production rehearsal plan as such. Again, it is important that the music be introduced with or around the same time as the choreography. Give students a copy of the vocal score in which they can make pencil notations. They need to learn the music as well as every other component of the show. Have the students mark notes in the notebook accordingly. Plan out the music rehearsals as you would any other rehearsal.

Choreography

Choreography rehearsals should be worked on after the vocal rehearsals have been run through. It is much easier for the cast to learn the moves to a song if they know the song first. "Throw out jazz hands on the word star." They'll retain the moves more if they can be related to a song that they are familiar with, either though previous experience or newly taught music.

Make sure the choreographer warms the students up prior to teaching movement and watch to see how the kids are handling the rehearsal. If they need to stop for water, rest, or simply take a break so everything soaks in, make sure this happens. Watch the rehearsal to see which actors are picking up the moves the fastest. The choreographer, being so engrossed in the music and movement, may not notice this, and it could be helpful for you to help pair up those who are catching on with those who are struggling. At least get the ones who are getting it out in front so that the others can watch. Encourage the students to use the choreography section of this book to jot down notes to be used during the home rehearsals. Plan choreography rehearsals as any other lesson plan.

Summary

Directors have an important role in making sure their vision of the script is portrayed on stage, all components of the show are in place, and everyone grows because of the experience. This book will help organize time and energy so that both directors and actors can get "on with the show!"

Chapter 4

Reproducibles

The following reproducibles are designed to help you to organize your rehearsals so that they are effective. It is suggested that directors reproduce this section of the book, keep it in a binder or folder, and use it throughout the rehearsal process.

DR1 Audition Announcement! Calling All Performers!

Show title: _____

Seeking youth in grades: _____

Produced by: _____

Artistic director: _____

Director: _____

Performance date(s): _____

Audition date(s): _____

Location: _____

Mandatory pre-audition meeting date(s) and time: _____

Location of mandatory pre-audition meeting: _____

Please attend this mandatory pre-audition meeting (with your parent[s] or guardian[s]) where you will meet the director, learn about the show, receive audition preparation materials, and be able to ask any questions you have about auditions, rehearsals, and the show.

Registration for Pre-audition Meeting

Name: _____   Phone: _____

Address: _____   City/Zip: _____

E-mail: _____

Deadline to hand in registration to audition: _____

Please contact us for audition registration forms and more specific information about the show.

Contact Information

Name: _____ Phone: _____ Hours: _____

Address: _____

E-mail: _____   Web site: _____

DR2   Pre-audition Meeting Materials List

What to Bring	Amount to Bring	Gathered	Notes
Agendas			
Samples of Script			
Volunteer Sign-up Sheet			
Sample of Music			
Equipment to Play Music			
Synopsis of Show			
Casting Needs Sheet			
Crew Information Page and Bios			
Audition Information			
Rehearsal and Production Schedule			

DR3   Pre-audition Meeting Agenda

Production title:

I. Show/production information (see separate handout)

   a. Title:

   b. Synopsis:

   c. Character numbers/casting needs:

   d. Run length:

   e. History:

   f. Goals for show:

   g. Costume requirements:

II. The crew

   a. Producer:

   b. Artistic director:

   c. Director:

   d. Stage manager:

   e. Choreographer:

   f. Vocal director:

   g. Technical director:

   h. Costume director:

   i. Props director:

   j. Scenery director:

   k. Art director:

III. Auditions

   a. Procedure:

   b. Call backs:

   c. Materials:

   d. Expectations:

DR3   (Continued)

    e. Auditions:

    f. How cast:

    g. Posting:

IV. Production season

    a. Rehearsal schedule:

    b. Production dates, location:

    c. Costume meeting:

    d. Sneak peak date, explanation:

    e. Script info:

V. Production policies

    a. Description/explanation:

    b. Questions:

VI. Other

    a. Volunteer sign-up:

    b. Questions:

DR4   Production Information

Show title: _____

Production season

    Rehearsal dates: _____

    Production dates: _____

Name: _____ Contact information: _____

Producer/producing organization: _____

Artistic director: _____

Co-director: _____

Assistant director: _____

Stage manager: _____

Technical director: _____

Costume director: _____

Makeup director: _____

Scenery director: _____

Props director: _____

Publicist: _____

Design director: _____

DR5   Production Policies

For the good of the production, as well as the individual cast members and cast and crew as a whole, the following policies will be upheld and apply to the entire cast. Please review the policies with your parent(s) or guardian and sign and return the policy form by the first rehearsal. Thank you.

- Participation in auditions commits the student to the part granted to him/her unless otherwise stated prior to auditions.

- Directors have the right to make decisions and changes as they see fit throughout the show for the betterment of the production.

- Cast members are expected to attend all required scheduled rehearsals.

- In the event of an absence from a rehearsal, the cast member is to notify the director.

- After more than three absences from rehearsals, the cast member will be put on probation.

- After more than four tardy entrances into rehearsal, the cast member will be put on probation.

- Casting decisions are based on performance at auditions and information provided at auditions by auditioner. Parts are earned through auditions and are not in any way granted due to past participation in a production, parent involvement, or other outside factors not related to the performance seen by the judges at the audition.

_____   _____
Signed (parent/guardian)   Date   Signed (student)   Date

DR6   Character Involvement Chart

Character	Dialogue Involvement	Singing Involvement	Characteristics	Choreography Involvement	Scenes Involved In	Notes

DR7   Actor Audition Information

Name: _____   Age: _____   Grade: _____

School: _____   Phone: _____

E-mail for correspondence purposes: _____

Address: _____   City: _____   Zip: _____

Role(s) you are auditioning for (optional): _____

Strengths you feel you possess that would enhance your participation in the show:

_____

_____

_____

___ I would like to participate in any role given to me. My greatest desire is to be in this production.

___ I would like to be cast as one of the above parts. Please do not consider me for other roles.

Experiences relating to this opportunity: _____

_____

_____

Photo attached on back: _____ yes   Date photo was taken: _____

Please list three physical characteristics that you think stand out most and will enhance your part in the production: _____

_____

_____

Please list the three personality characteristics that you think stand out most and will enhance your part in the production: _____

_____

_____

You may also submit a resume with this audition information page.

DR8 Rehearsing for Auditions: Students

Date of audition: _____ Today's date: _____

Number of days for preparation: _____

I will rehearse at _____ every day for _____ minutes.

Information on part: _____

_____

_____

1. What I know about the part I'm auditioning for: _____

_____

_____

2. Who is this character? _____

_____

_____ Age? _____

What does she/he like? _____

_____

_____

What does she/he dislike? _____

_____

_____

What do I need to do in auditions to portray this character? _____

_____

_____

What specific characteristics make this character interesting? _____

_____

_____

3. Notes: voice inflection, facial expression, movement, responses to other stimuli:

_____

_____

DR8   (Continued)

4. The responses from the character I will be speaking to (in theory): _____

_____

_____

5. The responses from the character I will be singing to: _____

_____

_____

6. Comments: _____

_____

_____

DR9 Casting Audition Rating Chart

Audition judges: Please use this chart to record notes about auditioning actors and to compare results.

Rating scale: 1 = low, 3 = average, 5 = above average

Auditioner	Grade/ Age	Auditioning For	Dialogue (Clarity, Enunciation, Expression)	Singing (Pitch, Tempo, Expression)	Movement, Coordination, Rhythm, Accuracy, Energy	Confidence/ Poise	Overall Preparation	Total Rating Score

DR10   Audition Slip

Audition slip for: _____

Number (order in which you will audition): _____

_____ Auditioned   _____ Please remain in the waiting room until called back this evening.

_____ Please plan on coming to callbacks at _____ on _____.

_____ Your audition for this evening has concluded. You may leave. Thank you for auditioning.

**Note: Audition results will be posted at _____ by _____. If you are cast in the show, we will send a commitment letter to you no later than _____ and it must be signed and submitted by _____. Failure to do so will exclude you from the cast.

As discussed at the pre-audition meeting, you may accept or decline any casting offer you receive. Should our talent base decline the opportunities offered to them, the show may be canceled due to casting limitations. This will be beyond our control.

Notes:

DR11   Actor Involvement Chart

Once you have cast your show, fill in the chart below. Use this information to map out rehearsals and to determine which actors are required at each rehearsal. Share the chart with the cast so that they are clear on their involvement in the play/musical.

Actor	Cast As	Singing Involvement	Scenes Involved In	Notes

DR12   Casting Letter

Dear _____,

Congratulations! We are pleased to inform you that you have been cast as _____
_____ in the upcoming production of _____
_____.

   The audition judges assessed what each individual actor displayed at the auditions and cast the actors in the roles according to what would best fit what we, as the directors, are looking for in each character. If you are committed to accepting this role, please fill in the information and mail it to _____ no later than _____.
Please plan on attending the first rehearsal, as stated in the pre-audition materials. You will be receiving your rehearsal materials at that time.
   Again, congratulations and welcome to the cast! We look forward to working with you!

Sincerely,

_____
Artistic Director

. . . . please print . . . .

I, _____, accept the role of _____ in the

production of _____.

Signed _____   Date _____

DR13   Casting Decline Letter

Dear _____,

Thank you for auditioning for a part in the upcoming production of _____.

The judges assessed what each individual actor displayed at the auditions and cast the actors in the roles according to what would best fit with what the directors are looking for in each character.

Unfortunately, due to the large number of students who auditioned for the show, we were unable to cast you in a part in this production.

Although this must be disappointing to you, take comfort in knowing that you gained a valuable experience through auditioning, which will undoubtedly help you at your next audition. Please remember—*if you haven't been selected to be a part of the show, it does not mean that you aren't talented.* Many famous actors have not received certain parts simply because they didn't "fit" in a particular role in a production based on the directors' vision of the show. These same actors were cast in different shows in lead roles because the director felt it was a better fit.

In conclusion, I'd like to thank you for auditioning and congratulate you on your participation.

Sincerely,

_____
Artistic Director

DR14   Commitment Contract

Show title: _____

Production season: _____

To: _____

From: _____

Congratulations! Based on audition results, you have been cast as _____ in our upcoming production. Accepting this part will commit you to all obligations related to participation in this production experience, including but not limited to attending all scheduled rehearsals and performances. Please sign this contract and return it to the director by _____.

I, _____, accept the opportunity to participate in this production in the capacity listed above. I will put forth my best effort and carry through this commitment until the conclusion of the production.

Signed (student) _____   Date _____

Signed (parent/guardian) _____   Date _____

DR15   Rehearsal Schedule

Date	Day of Week	Time	Rehearsal Plan	Cast Required	Location	Preparation for Rehearsal	Materials to Bring

DR16 Director's Rehearsal Plans

Show title: _____

Day: _____ Date: _____

Time: _____ Act: _____

Scenes _____ to _____

Objectives	To Target	Materials	Notes
1.			
2.			
3.			
4.			
5.			
6.			
7.			
8.			
9.			
10.			
Character notes	Follow up from previous rehearsal	Follow up for next rehearsal	

DR17   Rehearsal Plans at a Glance

Show title: _____

Day:	Day:	Day:	Day:
Date:	Date:	Date:	Date:
Crew:	Crew:	Crew:	Crew:
Covering:	Covering:	Covering:	Covering:
Type:	Type:	Type:	Type:
Objectives	Objectives	Objectives	Objectives
1.	1.	1.	1.
2.	2.	2.	2.
3.	3.	3.	3.
4.	4.	4.	4.
Notes:	Notes:	Notes:	Notes:

DR18a Type of Rehearsal Plans

To ensure that you budget your time accordingly, use this chart to plan out the types of rehearsals you will be calling, indicating what you would like to accomplish at each, the date, times, and so on. The following is a list of rehearsal types to consider in your planning.

Rehearsal Type	Number of Each Type Needed
Read-throughs	
Lyric Music Intro	
Blocking and Stage Map	
Choreography	
Vocal/Music	
Off Book	
Sneak Peak	
Run-through	
Dress Rehearsals	
Tech Rehearsals	
Pick-up	
Production Runs	

DR18b   Rehearsal Lesson Plans

Show title: _____

Type of Rehearsal	Objectives	Length Needed	Materials	Cast Involved	Act and Scenes	Dates	Times

DR19   Vocal Rehearsal Plans

Show title: _____

Date: _____

Act: _____ Scene: _____ Song: _____

Cast involved: _____

Measure(s)	Characterization	Stage Business	Blocking	Props Involved
1.	1.	1.	1.	1.
2.	2.	2.	2.	2.
3.	3.	3.	3.	3.
4.	4.	4.	4.	4.
5.	5.	5.	5.	5.
6.	6.	6.	6.	6.
7.	7.	7.	7.	7.
8.	8.	8.	8.	8.
9.	9.	9.	9.	9.
10.	10.	10.	10.	10.

Notes:

DR20   Blocking Rehearsal Plans

Show title: _____

Day: _____   Date: _____   Time: _____

Act: _____   Scene(s): _____   Script pages: _____

Characters involved: _____

Tempo: _____

Set demands: _____

Stage Map with Set

Blocking Steps	Materials	Stage Map	Characters
1.			
2.			
3.			
4.			
5.			
6.			
7.			
8.			

Blocking Chart

upstage center
stage right　　　　center stage　　　　stage left
downstage center

DR22   Choreography Rehearsal Plans

Show title: _____

Day: _____ Date: _____ Time: _____

Act: _____ Scenes: _____ Song: _____

Libretto pages: _____

Characters involved: _____

Tempo: _____ Set demands: _____

Stage Map with Set

Choreography Steps	Materials	Stage Map	Characters
1.			
2.			
3.			
4.			
5.			
6.			
7.			
8.			

DR23　Director's Notes for Cast Members

Have a page for each actor to keep track of progress. Share this with the actor often.

	Date Noted	Solid	Needs Work	Date Due for Improvement	Notes
Memorization					
Acting					
Characterization					
Staying in Character					
Line Delivery					
Stage Business					
Blocking					
Choreography— Accuracy					
Choreography— Presentation					

DR24 Director's Notes for Scenes

Act/Scene	Area that Needs Work	Cast Involved	Coached	Action Taken	Follow Up	Notes

DR25 Run-through Notes

This is it—the last-minute opportunity to fix the little details of the show before the curtain call. Take careful notes and share them with the actors after rehearsals.

Act:

Scene	Note	Character(s) Involved	Action Taken	Follow Through
1				
2				
3				
4				
5				
6				
7				
8				
9				
10				
11				
12				

DR26   Script Page

Scene	Stage Direction	Blocking	Choreography	Vocal	Lights	Sound

DR27 Script Preparation Abbreviation Codes

Use this page to code your script, indicating blocking, entrance/exit notes, and other directions for the play.

ESRt—enter stage right

ESLt—enter stage left

ExSRt—exit stage right

ExSLt—exit stage left

SmUStLt—stage movement upstage left

SmUStRt—stage movement upstage right

SmDstRt—stage movement downstage right

SmDstLt—stage movement downstage left

CrStRt—cross stage right

CrStLt—cross stage left

Ch—choreography

V—vocal

Lit—light

Crtn—Curtain

Scnry—Scenery

Snd—Sound

Section 2

The Actor's Handbook

Preparing for auditions, being cast, learning your part, rehearsing choreography, memorizing lines, working on blocking . . . all are a part of the preparation for a show. But how do you actually accomplish this daunting work? The student section of this book will give you step-by-step advice to help you prepare so that when the curtain goes up, you are truly ready to hit the stage.

Chapter 1

Auditions

This chapter contains suggestions on how to prepare for auditions as well as advice on what to do during auditions. You are encouraged to complete the exercises interspersed throughout this section as part of the preparation for auditions.

Auditions are stressful. Almost everyone gets nervous when they have to audition, even the most seasoned actor. And it makes sense to get the jitters because you are alone on a stage, asked to sing, dance, or act in front of people who are judging you. But don't worry, there are many tips that can help you relax a bit and actually enjoy the process.

Preparing for the Audition: Rehearsing at Home

Being well prepared for auditions will not only help you become less nervous, but it will also help you do your very best at auditions. Whether you have audition materials to prepare with or are going into auditions "cold" (without materials to work with), you will need to spend some time at home preparing. Determine how much time you have before auditions and rehearse every day until the day arrives. Make sure you aren't cramming the night before auditions. You might find it helpful to give yourself some at-home rehearsal notices so that you can schedule when you are going to rehearse and for how long. Your director may have provided you with a rehearsal planning form at the pre-audition meeting.

Rehearsing for Auditions

Date of audition: _____ Today's date: _____

Number of days for preparation: _____

I will rehearse at _____ every day for _____ minutes.

Acting for Auditions

The first step in preparing for auditions is to think about the character(s) in the show that you will be auditioning for. Do a "character study" for the characters in the show. Ask yourself these questions: How would this character think? How would he or she move? How would he or she talk? What makes him or her happy? What upsets him or her? Your goal is to *become* the character on stage so you must get to know this character. Do the best you can with whatever information you have. The audition prep work exercise can help with this.

If you don't have any idea about the characters in the show, simply portray yourself during auditions. Let the auditors see your self-confidence up on stage. Demonstrate how you are able to move and say your lines with self-esteem. Show your energy. Show them how well prepared you are. This is what the auditors will be impressed with.

When at home rehearsing, make sure you aren't just "memorizing" lines for auditions. Judges aren't interested in hearing a dull, lifeless reading of a part. Anyone can memorize. And depending upon the judges, it is often okay to use your script during auditions. Some recommend holding on to them on stage in case you do forget your lines. It's a lot better to glance at the script during a reading than to blank out and panic on stage.

Audition Prep Work

Fill in the following information to help you prepare for auditions.

Information that I have on the part of: _____

Who is this character? _____

What I know about the part I'm auditioning for: _____

_____

Age: _____

What the character likes: _____

What the character dislikes: _____

What I need to do in auditions to portray this character: _____

_____

The responses from the character I might be speaking with on stage during auditions:

_____

_____

Notes: voice inflection, facial expression, movement, responses to other characters and events.

Vocal Preparation for Auditions

Songs need to be sung accurately during auditions so that the judges know you can carry this through to show time. Sing in tune, and get the tempo and the rhythm right. If you know music, you'll be able to do this. If you don't, you should get some help. Your parents, the music teacher at school, a choir director, or even a friend can help out. You may want to contact the organization with whom you are auditioning with to see if they offer audition workshops or private vocal lessons.

While you are singing on stage, make sure to act the song out. In a musical, a major part of the story is portrayed through the music, so singing a song is part of the storytelling. When rehearsing the song, first learn the language of the music (again, the tempo, rhythm, pitch changes, and so forth). Know the song well and hit every note accurately. Determine if it is best to use your chest voice or your head voice.

Once the music is learned, it is time to study the lyrics. What is the song about? What type of emotions should you be portraying when singing the song as the character? What type of emotions are you trying to evoke from the audience? You need to carry the characteristics of the role you are playing into the song. If the character you are portraying is a person in mourning, don't sing the song with a grin—it wouldn't fit the emotion of the scene. Rather, get up on stage and sing the song as someone sad would sing it. This is easier for some than for others.

Other questions to ask yourself: Who is the character singing to? Why is he or she singing to that person (or animal or object)? Once you develop the story in your mind, allow that other character to come to life, too. Picture the reactions to each word you sing, and play off of that imaginary reaction. In other words, if you are singing a song that gives sad news to the imaginary character, you would show this emotion on stage. Remember, you are an actor as well as a singer. When you are practicing at home, make sure the imaginary character is in the room with you every time you sing. This will teach you to sing with more character portrayal, giving your auditors a more interesting and believable performance to judge. Complete the following exercise, which is a chart on preparing for vocal auditions.

Rehearsing for a Vocal Audition

Date of audition: _____ Today's date: _____

Number of days for preparation: _____

I will rehearse at _____ every day for _____ minutes.

What I know about the song I'm auditioning for: _____

_____

What I need to do in auditions to portray the character that sings this song: _____

_____

Who is this character? _____

Age: _____

Rehearsing for a Vocal Audition   (Continued)

What she/he likes: _____

_____

What she/he dislikes: _____

_____

The primary emotion to act during this song: _____

To whom, if anyone, is the character singing? _____

The responses from the character I will be singing to: _____

Where this other character would be on stage: _____

Dynamics: Learn the dynamics of the songs that you are working on.

pp—very soft   p—soft   mp—medium soft
mf—medium loud   f—loud   ff—very loud
  <—increase loudness   >—decrease loudness   rit.—gradually slower

Notes: voice inflection, facial expression, movement, response to other characters and events.

Choreography for Auditions

You probably will not be taught the dance steps you will do at auditions prior to the actual auditions. Most likely you will be taught a set of moves at auditions. Keep yourself limber and practice moving in front of a mirror at home. Watch yourself in the mirror. How do you look? Are you full of energy? Make sure you don't look down at your feet. Keep a strong, good posture. Be aware of your facial expressions (you don't want to have your tongue sticking out when you are doing a line kick). Be in control of your body as well as your face. Run through the exercise on rehearsing choreography for auditions.

Choreography Rehearsal Plan for Auditions

When at home, and immediately before you attend auditions, do the following exercises. As with any physical movement, do so with doctor approval.

Stretch. Stretch out your legs, arms, and neck. Flex your hands, wrists, and ankles by moving them in circles repeatedly one direction and then the other. Stretch up on your toes, then bend at the waist, and touch your toes. Bend your knees gently and slowly stand up, leaving your knees bent.

Choreography Rehearsal Plan for Auditions   (Continued)

Facial Expression. Stand in front of the mirror. Express yourself as happy, sad, angry, confused, embarrassed, frustrated, and with joy. Learn what each of these feels like so that you can portray these expressions during your choreography numbers.

Envision the stage you will be performing on. Think about the space available during auditions. When performing choreography during auditions, although you don't want to lumber across the stage like an elephant (unless, of course, you are auditioning to be an elephant), it is wise to enjoy the movement and use big moves full of energy rather than tiny, reserved, stiff, or emotionless moves.

The stage map included here may be used to plan choreography auditions if you have been pre-taught the moves.

Stage Map

Name of Song: _____

upstage center

stage right   center stage   stage left

downstage center

Nailing the Audition

When you step on to the stage, make eye contact with the judges and wait until you have their signal to begin. Transform into the part, but again, don't over do it. When your audition is complete, don't charge off the stage. Thank the judges. Look them in the eye. When they have acknowledged you, leave at a normal pace.

Judges expect the auditioners to be nervous. But they also expect actors to be able to overcome this nervousness, or at least not to let it stand in the way of their act. On opening night, nerves will once again play a part in the whole picture. Actors who can overcome this nervousness during auditions are more likely to become a part of the cast.

Remember, this is your one chance to make a good first impression on the judges. Do your best. Even if you mess up—mix up a few words or stumble—a good judge can see through that and know of your true ability to fit their casting needs. So don't beat yourself up over a less than perfect audition.

What to Wear

Although you may think that dressing in character is the best way to show you can fit a particular character, some judges feel it is actually better to dress like yourself. Show respect—don't show up in cut-off jeans and tennis shoes—but don't overdress. If you are called back, make sure to wear your hair the same and dress in the exact same outfit you wore during your first audition. If you are auditioning for a group or an organization that you haven't worked with before, the judges won't know you. In a case such as this, sometimes an auditioner is simply referred to by what he or she is wearing. If you wear a brown sweater to the first audition and a green polo shirt to the call back, that connection could be lost.

Your Attitude at Auditions

Do your best during the audition, but remember: the auditors are not there to judge *you* but rather your talent and what you show them at auditions. Their job is to sift through all of the actors to find the person that best fits the description of the character the director is seeking. Prepare for auditions as best you can, but remember that even the most prepared, talented actor may not be cast in a role if the director thinks it does not fit him or her. That's just show biz.

The more self-confident you are, the better you will come across to the auditors. An auditor will never cast an actor who looks so scared on stage that he or she is about to fall apart. It is too risky. So enjoy the moment, think of it as a learning experience, and prove to the director that you are right for the part. The more you believe in yourself and your abilities, the more you can convince others to do so as well.

Materials to Bring to Auditions

Often directors or audition judges ask actors to bring certain materials to the audition. You will probably be asked to bring a recent photo of yourself. Try to bring a photo that really looks like you. Don't bring one from last Halloween in which you are dressed up as Superman, even if that was your best hair day. Use the audition materials checklist to make sure you have the needed materials ready to go.

Audition Materials Checklist: What to Bring

Materials	Requested	Prepared to bring
Script	_____	_____
Music	_____	_____
Auditions registration info	_____	_____
Music	_____	_____
Photo	_____	_____
Resume	_____	_____
Monologue	_____	_____
Other	_____	_____

Accepting the Casting Decisions

Once auditions are completed and the roles are cast and posted, you need to accept what the auditors have decided. Trust the auditors. They have the best interest of the show in mind. It might hurt your ego but the more graciously you accept it, the more you will grow as an actor and a person.

Lastly, but most importantly, do your best with whatever part you receive, if you are indeed cast in the show. Each production, each part, each moment on stage is a new learning experience for you and will help you grow as an actor. Embrace it and do the best you possibly can. Not only for yourself, your fellow cast members, and your director, but also for the audience members who are counting on you to entertain them. Remember, "There are no small parts, only small actors."

Chapter 2

Getting the Most Out of Rehearsals

You've been cast in the show. Congratulations! Now, to learn your parts. This chapter will help you become an organized member of your cast. Although most actors focus on the production run itself, one of the most enriching segments of participating in a play or musical is really the journey to get there. A large part of the journey consists of the rehearsals with the cast. Making the most out of such time will improve the outcome of the show, and it will make it more enjoyable for you while helping you to become a better artist along the way.

Attendance

It is crucial that you attend every required rehearsal. You are part of the show; you made the commitment. The show can't go on without you. Even if you feel you have a small part, that part is an integral component of the show. Without you, the rest of the cast has to guess how you will handle the blocking, how long it will take for you to cross the stage, how loud you will be when you talk, and in what direction you will be looking when you deliver lines. It is too much to ask of your fellow cast members, let alone your directors, to miss rehearsals. Most actors look forward to rehearsals. It is a great way to spend their time because they love the art form and the comraderie that develops among cast and crew members. When you put forth your best effort and realize your importance to the show, you have that much better of a time. The show is better for it, too.

Rehearsal Schedule

Once you receive the rehearsal schedule from your director, study it carefully to know where you are to be and when. Also, if possible, know what you will be covering at each rehearsal. Come prepared. If you are to be on stage on Tuesday without scripts, acting your parts, it will slow up progress if you have not yet learned your lines and the director has to "line-feed" you. It will also frustrate the director and your fellow cast members. When you do receive your schedule, sit down with the rehearsal schedule form in your handbook and input all of the information. It is recommended that you take a highlighter pen and highlight the main deadlines, such as the "off script" deadline.

Within the schedule, make sure to write down what the director has planned so that you are aware of what you will be working on at each rehearsal.

Rehearsal Schedule

Date: _____	Date: _____	Date: _____	Date: _____
Time: _____	Time: _____	Time: _____	Time: _____
Location: _____	Location: _____	Location: _____	Location: _____
Type: _____	Type: _____	Type: _____	Type: _____
Materials needed:	Materials needed:	Materials needed:	Materials needed:
__Script	__Script	__Script	__Script
__Notes	__Notes	__Notes	__Notes
__Costume	__Costume	__Costume	__Costume
__Props	__Props	__Props	__Props
__Music	__Music	__Music	__Music
__Student	__Student	__Student	__Student
__Handbook	__Handbook	__Handbook	__Handbook

Director's Notes

Notes from directors are crucial because they override the script notes. It is important to jot down all notes that the director says and input them in your handbook. Do not rely on your memory for every blocking detail. Write them down so that you can review them at home during rehearsals. Do not, however, feel responsible for writing down notes about other characters unless they are directly related to you and what you will be doing on stage.

Script Preparation

Ah. You've finally been handed your script. Treat it like gold; keep it by your side as much as you can. Find out about the scripts—are they being rented from a company and need to be returned? If so, your options for writing in it are minimal—you can write very lightly in pencil, realizing that you will have to erase every mark prior to its return. Another option is to use Post-it Notes and place them on the margins of your script.

If the script is yours to keep, here are some ideas for preparing it for use. First, go through and highlight all of your parts. Next, write in the margins all notes from the director. Make sure to highlight in a different color all stage movement already indicated in the script that your director calls for. Take notes on everything possible that impacts your character, making a distinction between what you mark in your script and what you mark in your student handbook. Using abbreviations can make note taking easier (see supplied list).

Script Preparation Abbreviation Codes

Use this page to code your script, indicating blocking, entrance/exit notes, and other directions for the play.

ESRt—enter stage right

ESLt—enter stage left

ExSRt—exit stage right

ExSLt—exit stage left

SmUStLt—stage movement upstage left

SmUStRt—stage movement upstage right

SmDstRt—stage movement downstage right

SmDstLt—stage movement downstage left

CrStRt—cross stage right

CrStLt—cross stage left

Ch—choreography

V—vocal

Lit—light

Crtn—Curtain

Scnry—Scenery

Snd—Sound

Come Prepared

When the director calls for the start of rehearsal, you should be prepared. You should have the confidence to run through the blocking, lines, choreography, or vocals because you have rehearsed them at home and you know your stuff. Take care not to over rehearse or sound memorized. Further, do not work ahead; the director may make changes and then you will have rehearsed something that no longer is as it was.

Choreography

Choreography is the movement to music that adds life to the musical. The choreography should be visually appealing for the audience as well as help to tell the story.

Choreography is somewhat challenging to document. You learn the moves and really need to retain it in your memory on the spot. However, there are a few tips on how and what to jot down so that you can go home knowing that you will be rehearsing the moves correctly.

First, have a copy of either the music or lyrics. Next, indicate a movement at the word or musical measure that it occurs. Go through and put that same movement down for each repeated time. If there is a move you are to do specifically that does not follow the general cast, mark that down as well. This plan, as well as the stage map, should help you when rehearsing the choreography. Use a page for each song in the musical you will be participating in.

Stage Map

A stage map will help you to get a visual idea of where things will be happening on stage. When using the map, indicate areas on it by code (see list of abbreviations). This will make taking notes for movement pattern so much easier and less time consuming. These are the same codes you used for your script, so you should be familiar with them. You should use the stage map for each scene in the musical.

Stage Map

Act _____ Scene _____

upstage center

stage right   center stage   stage left

downstage center

Movement Patterns

Movement patterns are the map of movement for each character. A director might create your movement pattern to travel upstage right and lean against a prop, then direct you to sing a solo, in the spotlight. It is up to you to learn your own movement pattern. Take notes during rehearsal.

Blocking and Stage Business

Blocking and stage business—planning and learning where you will be on stage, when, and in what manner—is a large part of the production. It is as essential to learn the blocking and stage business as it is to learn your lines and memorize choreography. When learning blocking, think about it in terms of what makes sense for the show. The director gives blocking direction based on the interpretation of the story, so it should make sense and, therefore, should allow you to learn it easier. Indicate in your script where you enter, exit, stand, sit, and so on. Make careful notes of all so when you are at home, you can go over them as often as you need to. Use the blocking chart to assist you with your notes.

Blocking Chart		
upstage center		
stage right	center stage	stage left
downstage center		

Rehearsal Checklist

Prior to attending a rehearsal, go through the checklist to make sure you are well prepared and ready to accomplish the most you can at practice.

Getting into Character. You are transforming into your character the moment you step onto the stage for rehearsal. No matter how smooth the rehearsal is running, are you staying in character, concentrating, and taking notes when needed?

Line Reading. Do you have your dialogue memorized? Do you know your lines, when they are to be delivered, and where you are to be on stage?

Choreography. Do you know where you are to be and the moves you are to perform? If this was reviewed in class, it is your responsibility to retain it to memory. The faster you do this, the more time the cast will have to perfect the finer points of the show. Make sure during rehearsals that you pay close attention to the choreographer. Notice not only his or her movements, but also where the hands are, the way the head is positioned, where he or she is looking, the amount of energy used to execute each move, and the like. All of these elements are what make the choreography complete. Mark down any notes that will help you remember what you are expected to learn so you can rehearse the moves and patterns at home.

Chapter 3

At-Home Rehearsals

Although rehearsals with the cast are crucial, equally important is the time you put into rehearsing on your own. It is during this time that you can hone your specific responsibilities of the show and make sure you do your best.

At-Home Rehearsal Schedule

Organizing your time at home so that you can adequately rehearse is an important key to a successful show. Your at-home rehearsal schedule should be coordinated with your personal schedule. It is important to set aside time to rehearse just like you do for math homework or practicing piano. Choose a time when you will be fresh and able to concentrate, and pick a spacious, quiet place in your home, preferably with a mirror. Rehearsing with a friend, sibling, or parent is helpful during certain parts of the at-home rehearsal process, so plan a time that you will be able to count on others to help out. Use the at-home rehearsal plan and checklist to schedule and keep track of these things.

At-Home Rehearsal Plan

Date	Date	Date	Date	Date	Date
Time designated	Time designated	Time designated	Time designated	Time designated	Time designated
Rehearsal location	Rehearsal location	Rehearsal location	Rehearsal location	Rehearsal location	Rehearsal location
Materials needed	Materials needed	Materials needed	Materials needed	Materials needed	Materials needed

At-Home Rehearsal Plan   (Continued)

Focus of rehearsal	Focus of rehearsal	Focus of rehearsal	Focus of rehearsal	Focus of rehearsal	Focus of rehearsal
Act: Scene: Song:	Act: Scene: Song:	Act: Scene: Song:	Act: Scene: Song:	Act: Scene: Song:	Act: Scene: Song:
Notes	Notes	Notes	Notes	Notes	Notes

At-Home-Rehearsal Checklist

Keep this checklist handy and indicate when you have completed each section of the checklist.

_____ Read through script

_____ Do storyline outline

_____ Highlight your parts in the script if your director gives you permission to mark up your book

_____ Do the character study found in your student handbook

_____ Always begin by warming up

_____ Recite your parts with expression, motivation, and understanding

_____ Memorize your lines/songs

_____ Master the choreography

_____ Know your part off-book

Warm-up Exercises

Prior to each rehearsal at home, it is important to warm up both your body as well as your voice. Here are a few tips to help you get warmed up.

Vocal Warm-up. Form your lips in the shape of an "o" and say "ooo." You will now sing "ooo" by sliding your voice up and down the scale in a siren like manner. Allow your mouth to open as you go up the scale. Let your breath come in naturally, and sing on the exhalation like you are blowing out a candle.

Facial Warm-up—Mirror play. Study your character and determine the types of emotions your character should portray throughout the show. Write these down. Then, in front of a mirror, create this "mood" through facial expressions. When you feel satisfied with this, ask a family member or friend to guess the type of emotions you are trying to portray. If he or she guesses them all correctly, you are on the right track with your character portrayal.

Physical Warm-up. Make sure you warm up your muscles prior to doing choreography. For more information on warm-ups, check with your physical education teacher or doctor.

Learning to Act Your Part

Memorization is a critical part of being in a production. You must, without a doubt, memorize your lines. It is embarrassing to get up on stage and then have lines fed to you from behind the side curtain. Further, it is quite stressful to be up on stage searching your mind, in a panic, to come up with the right line at the right time. The bottom line is that you should understand the story. The story is what the audience wants. They come to see the talent, no doubt, but it is the story, the emotion the story evokes, that will captivate the audience. True, there are times when the story isn't as interesting as the fantastic actors, singers, or dancers on stage. But in a solid production, the director will have chosen a play or musical that fits the intended audience.

While memorizing lines is important to portray the story, keep in mind that memorization is also somewhat dangerous. For although you want to learn your lines perfectly so that you won't forget them, if you sound memorized it will take the umpf out of your performance. The goal is to act like what is taking place on stage is really happening in true life. No one in real life spits back lines from a script.

There is one trick in preventing the "memorization dialogue" from happening, but it has two parts. First, make sure to get into character whenever you are rehearsing. *Never* just say your lines. *Always* act them. You must learn to act like you feel this way throughout your line reading. With practice, it will soon become second nature. Second, hold off trying to memorize by just reading through the script. This may sound simple and also boring: "Oh, I know what the script is about, we've gone over it in rehearsal. Let me just get *to my* part." You must keep in mind that the whole show *is* your part. You are a crucial part of the story, and your lines are a way of helping to get the whole story across. So start from the beginning and read the script through carefully as you would a novel for a book report. Pay attention to what you are reading. Understand exactly what is happening in the play or musical. Now put the script away. You are done for the time being.

When some time has passed, go back again to the script, open it up, and read through the script from the beginning. Now that you are more familiar with the story, what is happening first, second, and third? What is the conflict? How is it resolved? Where does the tension increase? Where is the climax of the story? Who are the main characters, and how do they react to the situations? Have another person spot check you—have that person read from the script and periodically stop to ask you what happens next.

The goal is to memorize the entire story so that it makes sense to you. This doesn't mean memorizing everyone else's lines, but rather, knowing the story well enough to know what happens first, second, third, and so forth. The best actors on stage are the ones who are very familiar with the entire script, and who can keep the story going even if there is a misdelivered line, a line delivered out of sequence, if someone skips a line, and the like. The actors on stage can improvise and throw in a line to get the cast going back in the right direction simply because they know the story. When it is your turn to deliver a line, even if you can't remember the exact words of the script, you can know the story well enough to say something that makes sense and moves the story forward. This method also helps you to deliver lines with feeling.

After you have completed your read-through, jot down the information on the storyline outline form to help you to retain the storyline. If you are unable to answer the questions without looking back, reread the entire script and try again.

Storyline Outline

Setting

Time of year: _____

Time of day: _____

Day of week: _____

Characters

Main: _____

Secondary: _____

Extras: _____

Problem

Conflict: _____

Climax: _____

Resolution: _____

Getting into Character

As discussed earlier, one of the most important aspects of rehearsing for a show is learning your part in character. Beyond memorization, actors must convince their audience that they truly are the character they are portraying in the show. Therefore, they must remain in character every moment they are on stage, whether it is their turn to recite dialogue or whether they are extras in a scene.

You may have the opportunity to act as an understudy. Treat this position as if you were cast in the part from the start. Many a star has been born when an actor had to step in and take over as an understudy because the lead was unable to come through. No matter what the part, study, rehearse, and be prepared.

To accomplish strong characterization, complete the characterization study prior to learning your lines.

Character Study

Character's name: _____

Character's age: _____

Character's gender: _____

Describe the way your character thinks: _____

Acts: _____

Moves: _____

Looks like: _____

Feels: _____

Who he/she interacts with: _____

Character traits—strengths: _____

Things the character hates: _____

Things the character loves: _____

Character traits—flaws: _____

Describe your character. Include everything you know about him/her as if you are telling someone about your best friend.

_____

_____

_____

_____

_____

1. Notes: voice inflection, facial expression, movement, response to other stimuli

2. The responses from the character I will be speaking to

Comments

Vocal Rehearsal Plan

You are at home and you need to work on your solo. How do you begin? First, make sure your voice is warmed up. When that is completed, take out your music and begin. Do you know the parts you will be singing? If you can read music, your challenge will be less because you can pick out the notes you are to sing on the piano. If not, hopefully you have learned it well enough during rehearsal or you have a recording of the music to rehearse with.

Begin by going over the lyrics. Read what the song is about, what you are to be thinking about, and what you are to be portraying. What part of the story are you telling? What stage business will your character be doing? (Your director will most likely help you with the blocking and stage business.) Get into character for your rehearsals, and learn how to "act" the song as well as you sing it. It is unsettling to watch a musical move along and then have the story come to a standstill because the music is sung and not acted. The song study exercise can help you focus on what you need to do.

If you are having trouble learning your music at home, make sure to tell your director, who may schedule individual time for you to rehearse with the music director or have the name of a private vocal director you can hire.

If you are rehearsing songs that you are singing in the chorus, it is equally important to know the meaning of the songs and to sing with expression.

Make sure to sing the parts as your music director has explained, noting the musical notations in the music so that the music is sung the way it was intended to be. It can't be stressed enough that the songs in a musical need to be as polished and well rehearsed as any part of the dialogue.

Song Study

1. Listen to the song, either by live or recorded performance.
2. Read the lyrics.

   a. What is the song about?

   b. Who is the song being sung to?

   c. Why is the song being sung?

   d. What is the character feeling while singing this song?

   e. How should the character look when singing this song?

3. Learn the music.
4. Learn the lyrics with meaning.
5. Rehearse the song with meaning, full characterization, and expression.
6. What is the stage business to be done while singing the song?
7. What is the blocking for the song?
8. Dynamics—learn the dynamics of the songs that you are working on.

pp—very soft	p—soft	mp—medium soft
Mf—medium loud	F—loud	ff—very loud
<—increase loudness	>—decrease loudness	rit.—gradually slower

Choreography Rehearsal Plan

It may be tempting to forgo rehearsing the choreography at home by yourself. After all, how much can you accomplish in a kick-line when you are the only kicker? A lot. You need to know your moves exactly, despite what others are doing. If you are able to concentrate on what you are doing and if someone makes a mistake during a song, you will have your wits about you to pull them back on track, just by leading by example. Get in front of the mirror. Learn the gross motor moves. Then, when you are well prepared, focus on all of the finer details of the choreography. How are your hands to be for each move? Are you smiling? Does your face portray the mood of the song? Are you sharp? Remember, in a musical production, the songs are a major part of the storytelling, so they are as important to moving the story along as the dialogue. You must deliver the song as you deliver the lines—with the correct mood. Is the song emotional? Full of energy? Learn the moves, sharp and clean, and then make sure you know how to act the song as well. Fill out the choreography rehearsal plan for each song you are dancing to.

Choreography Rehearsal Plan

Name of song: _____

1. Listen to the music.

2. Understand the words.

3. What type of energy should be portrayed while moving to this song? _____

   _____

4. What type of facial expression? _____

5. Body expression: _____

6. Do the moves in front of a mirror. Once the gross motor movements are learned, focus on the details—positions of hands, fingers, shoulders, and chin; direction of face, hips, and shoulders.

Strengthening Skills at Home

Acting is a skill to practice like anything else. You practice piano lessons, you learn your math facts, you study your geography. Find time to practice your acting skills outside of rehearsing for the production. There are a number of books available that have drama exercises in them. You can find them in educational stores, in book stores, in the library, and online. Look for resources that are age- and grade-appropriate. These games can be a fun way to spend time with family and friends while building skills in the arts.

Improvisation

What happens when you are up on stage and the lights are on you and you forget a line? Do you panic? Blush? Do you search the audience, looking for help, offstage, on the wings, to your fellow cast members? Do you mutter, "Um . . ." You need to be as well prepared *not knowing* the script as you are *knowing* the script. In other words, if you know how to recover on stage, you will never be stuck in this situation. If you know you will never be stuck in that situation, chances are more likely that you never will be, for often the fear of freezing on stage is what provokes memory loss.

When going over lines at home, make sure that you learn the script really well. That doesn't just mean learning *your lines* really well; it means knowing *the story* really well. Have someone quiz you by giving you a few lines that aren't in the script but have the same general meaning. Rehearse recovering at home so that you have the self-confidence to realize this same thing can be done in front of a full audience. Working on improvisational exercises like this will build your self-confidence and help you become a more skilled actor.

Chapter 4

The Final Show and the Aftermath

The hours of rehearsal are over. Everything is set. In a matter of minutes the curtains will open. You see from backstage the flicker of lights; the house noise dies down. Silence. And that's when it hits you. The biggest stage fright you have ever experienced.

It may or may not happen like this, but chances are, no matter how experienced you are, you will feel nervous just before you go out on stage. The key is to put this nervous energy into the job at hand. Transform into character before setting foot on stage, and then move forward. Immerse yourself in the story. Don't let your mind play mistake scenes for you—don't think about what will happen if you trip, if you sneeze, if you drop a line. Just get into the story and stay there, and before you know it, you will be hearing grand applause and realize that your first show is already over.

How to Recover on Stage

We've gone over trying to improvise a line when someone has skipped or misspoken a line. Knowing the story line can help in recovery, but the most crucial part of recovery, believe it or not, isn't in what you say, but how you say it.

Picture the scenario. The play is moving along at a good pace. The audience is into the show, they are watching intently, you can't even hear a pin drop in the house. Suddenly, your mind goes blank. You have no idea what to say. You begin to search for your director out in the audience, you look offstage to your left, then your right, searching, pleading for a line reader to save you. Then you look to your fellow actors. You are uncomfortable, and before you know it, you slip and say, "Oh, what was I supposed to say again?" Then a short chuckle, a nervous laugh, and you blush. This is an actor's worst nightmare. It is also a director's worst nightmare, for not only will your director feel sorry for your embarrassment, but a small episode such as this can squelch the momentum. It can push enthralled audience members back to reality.

If you have a sudden lapse in memory and can't remember your lines, or if you deliver the wrong ones, be the actor that you are. Here is the true test of your talent. Don't show it on your face. Don't indicate it in your voice. Don't show it in your body language. Just keep the show moving. Remember, "The show must go on" means more than just the opening curtain—it means it must go on until the end. Come up with a line that makes sense in the story, deliver it, and move on.

If something unforeseen happens outside of line dropping—such as a prop falling, an animal actor acting up, or someone slipping—unless someone is seriously injured, do your best to keep the show moving. Don't draw attention to something that detracts from the momentum of the play or musical. You may want to discuss with your director prior to opening night the preference for handling mishaps. Remember, things happen. Everything from forgetting lines, crying, vomiting, slipping, props falling, lights going out, music going awry, to babies crying in the audience. The idea is to realize this is live theater and to do the best that you can with the unforeseen circumstances. This is what engenders respect for actors in live theater. And this is why your audience is sitting in front of you instead of sitting in a movie theater.

Supporting Your Fellow Cast Members and Crew

Although you have spent much time rehearsing on your own, keep in mind that a play or a musical is similar to a team sport. Each "player" adds to the team and the more team spirit, camaraderie, and support fellow actors provide for each other, the stronger the final show will be. Remember, there are always stars in the show, but the true stars are those who know that every member of the cast is important.

The Aftermath

After the show you will have many feelings, and you may be greatly relieved that it is over. You will be assessing how well it went, perhaps disappointed in yourself, thinking you could have done better. You may be pleasantly surprised at the size of the audience and their reaction to your performance. Most likely you will feel proud of yourself and your cast's accomplishments, and you will feel a bit sad that the whole experience is winding down.

Once the spotlights are turned off, life goes on as normal. The only thing left to do is recall your fond memories. Most likely, you have learned some valuable skills and the experience has made you a better actor, performer, dancer, and vocalist. You will be able to draw on this when you prepare for your next audition and rehearse for your next production.

Glossary

Audition: An opportunity for an actor to display his or her talents in order to be cast in a production or show.

Auditioner: A person who is trying out for a role(s) in a production.

Auditor: The person who makes casting decisions during auditions; the audition judge.

Blocking: Preplanned movements on stage executed by the actor.

Casting: Selecting actors to portray characters or roles in a production.

Casting decisions: The final decisions of which actor will portray which role in a production.

Characterization: Creating a believable role through portrayal of various dimensions of a character.

Character study: The study of developing a character to be portrayed accurately in a show.

Choreographer: The person who facilitates, plans, teaches, and directs the dance sequences in a production.

Choreography: The movement and dance in a musical production.

Complete run-through: A rehearsal that includes working through the entire production, with all components in place.

Costume: The dress or attire in a show that helps portray the character.

Dialogue: The conversation between characters on stage.

Director's notes: Information written down by the director about the actors or scenes to improve the show.

Dress rehearsal: A rehearsal in which all characters are in costume.

Facial expression: The manner in which a character portrays feelings and emotions through his or her face.

Home rehearsal: A rehearsal outside of the cast rehearsals.

Improvisation: Spontaneous acting without preplanning.

Lines: The text an actor is required to commit to memory.

Lyrics: The words of a song.

Memorization: Committing lines, lyrics, movement, or anything else to memory so that they can be recalled without the use of external resources.

Movement pattern: The plan of movement developed to be executed on stage during a production.

Music director: The person hired to teach and direct the musical numbers of a production.

Opening night: The first show with an audience in a production run.

Pantomime: The expression of a story or thought through facial and physical expression rather than sound or speaking.

Pick-up rehearsal: A rehearsal that was not planned; called in order to brush up on certain parts of a show.

Pre-audition meeting: A gathering called prior to auditions to impart information about the production, crew, staff, and the audition process.

Production policies: Rules and regulations set forth by the director or artistic director in order to produce a successful show.

Recover: To move back into the show when lines have been missed or misdelivered.

Rehearsal: The time devoted to practicing the show.

Rehearsal handbook: An organizational resource to guide actors through the rehearsal procedures so that they can get the most out of their time spent working on the show.

Run time: The amount of time it takes to complete a show.

Script: The story done in text that is the object of study for the production.

Stage business: The movement other than choreography the actor is directed to complete on stage to portray part of the story.

Stage map: The planned route for an actor to follow on stage.

Vocal director: The person who is hired to direct actors on the proper use of their voice in the show's songs.

Vocal rehearsals: Rehearsals dedicated to learning songs.

Vocal score: The book that contains the show's songs.

Bibliography

Alberts, David. *Rehearsal Management for Directors*. Portsmouth, NH: Heinemann, 1995.

Bestor, Sheri L. M. *Gifted and Talented Drama/Theatre Pilot Program*. Rhodium Records, 1991.

Heinig, Ruth Beall. *Creative Drama for the Classroom Teacher*. Englewood Cliffs, NJ: Prentice Hall, 1988.

Peithman, Stephen, and Neil Offen. *Guide to Publicity*. Portsmouth, NH: Heinemann, 1999.

———. *Stage Directions Guide to Musical Theatre*. Portsmouth, NH: Heinemann, 2002.

Rees, Mandy, and John Staniuna. *Between Director and Actor*. Portsmouth, NH: Heinemann, 2002.

Rubin, Janet E., and Margaret Merrion. *Creative Drama and Music Methods*. North Haven, CT: Linnet Professional Publications, 1996.

Shurtleff, Michael. *Audition*. New York: Bantam Books, 1978.

Silver, Fred. *Auditioning for the Musical Theatre*. New York: Penguin Books, 1985.

Vened, Christopher. *In Character*. Portsmouth, NH: Heinemann, 2000.

Wagner, Betty Jane, and Dorothy Heathcote. *Drama as a Learning Medium*. Washington DC: National Education Association Publication, 1976.

Waxberg, Charles S. *The Actor's Script*. Portsmouth, NH: Heinemann, 1999.

Index

Note: References to director reproducibles are indicated by (DR).

About the Author

Sheri L. M. Bestor is the founder of the production company Stagekids as well as the North Shore Academy of the Arts, Inc. (NSAA), a not-for-profit company offering opportunities in the visual, performing, and literary arts. She has served as the president, CEO, and performing arts director for NSAA, and has vast experience producing and directing musicals with children through NSAA/Stagekids and school districts as well as at the university level. She has worked as a consultant in the performing arts, developing and implementing programming. She is an experienced elementary teacher with a master's degree in curriculum and instruction. Sheri has published works of both nonfiction and fiction, for both adults and children. She and her family live in a small town in the Midwest.

www.ingramcontent.com/pod-product-compliance
Ingram Content Group UK Ltd.
Pitfield, Milton Keynes, MK11 3LW, UK
UKHW050148280225
455689UK00007B/99